The ABC's of Financial Education:

An alphabet introduction for people of all ages in training to be the next financial expert.

by Ralph Newsome, II

Edited by Tanya Morant

All rights reserved. No part of this book may be reproduced or transmitted in any form or by any means without written permission from the author.

Printed in USA

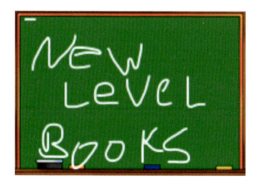

Copyright © 2020 Ralph Newsome, II

ISBN: 978-0-578-24108-1

A is for Assets

An asset is something you buy today with the hope that it will grow in value over time.

EXAMPLE: *Buy a house, let someone move in, and have them pay you money every month for allowing them to live in your house. You just turned your house into an asset.*

There are two asset categories:
- Paper assets and
- Physical assets

Examples of *paper assets* are buying stocks, bonds, and currencies.

Examples of *physical assets* are owning apartments/real estate, gold and silver, and owning businesses.

Assets put money in your pockets and liabilities take money out of your pockets.

ACTIVITY

Try making this into a song:

Assets feed you and liabilities eat you.
Dogs sniff you and trains go choo choo

2

B is for Budget

A budget is a key tool to help you manage your money; you will need to write down all your monthly expenses so you can keep track of how your money is being spent.

Do you know what an expense is? An expense is money that comes out of your pocket to buy things that you need or want.

EXAMPLE:

Your Expenses = $635 for the month

Category	Budgeted	Actual
Food	$ 100.00	$ 50.00
Clothes	$ 40.00	$ 35.00
Toys	$ 70.00	$ 100.00
School	$ 200.00	$ 200.00
Books	$ 100.00	$ 100.00
Sports	$ 50.00	$ 25.00
Electronics	$ 240.00	$ 125.00

The Budgeted column is the cost of what you planned to spend and the Actual column is what you really spent. The key is to have more money than expenses each month.

Tip! Track your spending each month for a every $ that you spend. No matter how small the purchase. Your goal is to spend less than the previous month.

BONUS! B is for Bonds

A bond is debt (see D) between the lender and borrower. The lender receives a fixed interest payment for lending the money to the borrower. The borrower uses the money from the lender to improve or expand their business.

There are several types of bonds:

1. Federal Government bonds called Treasury Bills (if held one year or less) or Notes (if held greater than one year)
2. Municipal bonds offered by states and municipalities
3. Corporate bonds offered by businesses. As an investor you can either buy stocks of a company or buy their bonds.
4. Agency bonds offered by government affiliated administrations

Tip!

Government bonds offered by the U.S.A. are known to be the safest investment in the world. In fact, they are considered to be so safe that they are called risk-free investments; however, with that safety you may also get a lower rate of return.

C is for Cash Flow

Cash Flow is the most important item of any business or individual. Cash flow is the money you receive for providing a good or service.

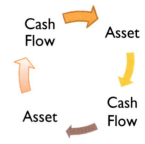

Whether that's working a job (which you provide your time) or working for yourself selling goods or services, cash flow is needed at a minimum, every month to help pay for things such as toys, clothes, or books.

> *Tip!* Your Cash Flow should also help you buy more assets that in return produce more cash flow. The picture above is a never-ending circle of buying assets which produces cash flow; the cash flow is then used to buy more assets, that produce more what? More cash flow! Nice Job!

BONUS! C is for Credit Score

A credit score is a three-digit number designed to represent your ability to pay your bills on time. It is extremely important to always keep a good credit score because credit (in today's world) = money and money = credit. The higher your credit score, the more money you can borrow. A good credit score is similar to receiving an A on a test. The better you do on a test shows how smart you are (well at least on that test). A better credit score shows how responsible you are about paying bills on time. Credit scores range from 350 to 850.

> *Tip!* Try to keep your credit score above 750 to be able to take advantage of the best interest rates available. Also safeguard your personal identifiable information such as your social security number like how Lebron guards his opponents.

D is for Debt

Debt is borrowed money. Credit and loans are other names for debt. Most debt is considered bad debt because the debt requires you to pay it back with your own money. Usually, the borrower will have to pay back the borrowed money (the principal) and pay back a little extra (the interest).

EXAMPLE: *You borrowed $100 from your parents. Your parents will want you to pay back the $100 you borrowed (the principal) and pay $10 for borrowing the money in the first place (the interest). $100 (principal) + $10 (interest) = $110.*

Did you know that debt can be tricky? Why? Debt can be tricky because sometimes people will borrow money to buy an asset (see A). This debt is considered *good debt* because the asset will pay for the debt you borrowed.

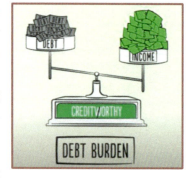

An example of *good debt* is buying a house to rent out to someone else. The tenant will pay you for living in your home. The money they pay to you will be used to pay the debt. You will not pay back the debt with your own money; instead you will use the money from someone else, in this case your tenant.

An example of *bad debt* is buying a car because you are paying the debt for the car using your own money.

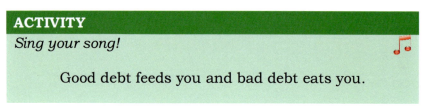

ACTIVITY
Sing your song!

Good debt feeds you and bad debt eats you.

E is for Economy

In simple terms, an economy is the measure of transactions.

Do you know what a transaction is? A transaction happens when you buy something using some form of money. The transaction that you purchased will provide either a "good" (something you can touch like toys or clothes) or a "service" (haircut/style or teacher/tutor). In return, the person or business that sold you the "good" or "service" receives the money. Then they turn around and buy a "good" or "service" from someone else and the process repeats itself a gazillion times. This drives the economy...**period**.

BONUS! *E is for Entrepreneur*

An entrepreneur is a person who creates their own business and helps creates jobs for others. Most big companies that you hear about today started with one individual or a team of people who had a vision to create a company. Phil Knight created Nike. Walt Disney created Disney. Bob Johnson created B.E.T. Jeff Bezos created Amazon.

F is for Fortnite (haha joking) *F is for the Federal Reserve System (The Fed)*

The Fed is America's central banking system. Most people believe The Fed is controlled by the government but it actually consists of privately owned banks, which are no different from Wells Fargo or SunTrust banks. The Fed controls the interest rate you pay, creates or controls inflation, and prints the money you have in pocket. So, it's safe to say that the people or businesses that own The Fed are the richest and most powerful people in the world!!

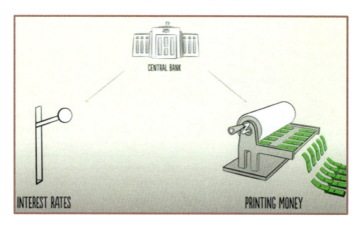

BONUS! *F is for Fiat Money*

Did you know the money supply that every country in the world prints today, even America, is actually fake money? The U.S. dollar was once backed by gold; once upon a time, we could go to a bank, give the teller a $20 bill, and in return get a gold coin. This is no longer the case and that's why our paper money is considered fake or fiat money. It has no actually value. The irony is we are all working, sweating, and fighting for monopoly money.

G is for Gold

Gold is real money. Every country in the world uses gold in some form or fashion.

Gold was used during biblical times, it is used today, and it will be used in the future.

 Ask for 1/10 ounce of gold for your birthdays, Christmas, etc. it will always hold its value.

H is for Home Equity

Home Equity is the difference between the value of a person's home and how much a person owes on the home.

EXAMPLE: *If your home is worth $400,000 and you owe $150,000, then you have home equity equal to $250,000. You would then be able to borrow against the $250,000 of equity in the form of a Home Equity Line of Credit (HELOC).*

Never use a HELOC to buy liabilities; only buy assets that will produce more what? More cash flow!

I is for Investor

An investor is a person who uses either their own income or debt to buy an asset. I'm sure you know what an asset is... right? Usually an investor is someone who buys an asset for long-term gains.

BONUS! I is for Income

Income is money you receive either from working a job or starting a business. Income is another term for cash flow. Cash flow is essential for survival for people and businesses.

DOUBLE BONUS! I is for Interest

Interest is the additional money you pay for borrowing money from someone else or borrowing money from a bank.

EXAMPLE: *If I borrow $100 from you and you charge me 10% interest, that means I have to pay you the $100 I borrowed (which is called the principal) plus $10 (which is the interest).*

$100 (principal) x 10% (interest) = $110.00

> **Tip!**
> Be the lender and not the borrower. You want to collect interest and not pay interest. Paying interest on items such as credit cards, car loans, student loans, etc. will make it hard to gain financial freedom.

TRIPLE BONUS! I is for Inflation

It is critical for you to understand inflation if you want to gain financial freedom. Inflation is a hidden tax on your money. A byproduct of inflation is higher prices on goods and services but that's because the value of the dollar goes down.

EXAMPLE: *A gallon of milk cost $0.49 in 1960, but today's milk is $3.99. So, let me ask you...did milk turn into gold since 1960 or did cows grow a fifth leg? **No!** So why did the price of milk go up so much? It's because the value of the dollar has gone down due to money printing. Because money is less valuable it takes more dollars to buy things today.*

J is for Joint Account

"DO YOU KNOW WHAT A BANK ACCOUNT IS?
A BANK ACCOUNT IS ISSUED BY A BANK WHO HOLDS YOUR MONEY IN A SAFE PLACE SO YOU DON'T HAVE TO WORRY ABOUT SOMEONE BREAKING INTO YOUR PIGGY BANK."

A JOINT ACCOUNT IS A BANK ACCOUNT (THINK OF YOUR PIGGY BANK) THAT TWO OR MORE PEOPLE CAN USE TOGETHER. YOU AND YOUR PARENTS OR GRANDPARENTS, OR UNCLES, OR AUNTS WOULD MAKE FOR A PRETTY AWESOME JOINT ACCOUNT.

K is for Key of David

This is less financial and more spiritual related. Having the "One" that owns the Key of David on your side will open all doors in all areas of life and will help you gain understanding.

L is for Landlord

A landlord is a title given to someone who owns real estate and then rents or leases the real estate to a person, a family, or a business. People who use the real estate pay the landlord every month.

BONUS! *L is for Liabilities*

A liability is money a person owes to someone else or a business. It can be in the form of debt (see D) or a one-time expense like buying a glue stick to fix a toy.

EXAMPLE: *Car loans, student loans, and credit card debt are all examples of liabilities because you owe money and you have to pay for the liabilities out of your own pocket.*

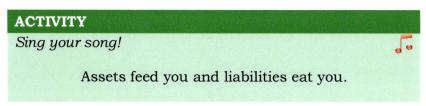

M is for Market

A market is a function of the economy (see E). A market brings buyers and sellers together to transact with one another usually to buy goods and services. This can be a physical market like a toy store or it can be an online market like eBay which is used to sell used goods.

EXAMPLE: *The stock market allows buyers to buy stocks of their favorite companies like Google and it also allows sellers to sell the shares of companies like Twitter to other buyers.*

There is a market for just about anything you can think of, like the Real Estate Market, Bond Market, Gold Market, Oil Market, Grain Market, Custom Sneakers Market, etc.

N is for Net Worth

Simply put: Net Worth = your Assets – your Liabilities.

🙌 Raise your hand if you know what an Asset is!

EXAMPLE: *If your toy business is worth $400,000 and you only have $150,000 in liabilities, your net worth would be $250,000.*

This metric will help you determine if you have too many liabilities and not enough assets. Banks like to see you with a higher net worth to be able to qualify for certain loans. So, try to buy more assets to increase your net worth.

ACTIVITY
Add a dance to go with your song!

Assets feed you and liabilities eat you.

O is for Opportunity Cost

Opportunity Cost represents missed opportunities based on a person's decision to pursue one investment strategy over another.

EXAMPLE: *If I pursue Opportunity A and it brings me a rate of return of 10% however, Opportunity B would have brought me a rate of return of 15%, then my opportunity cost would be 5% (15% -10% = 5%).*

Here's the Formula: MO (Missed Opportunity) – CO (Chosen Opportunity) = OC (Opportunity Cost)

Similarly, studying vs. watching TV is the opportunity cost between getting an A or getting an F.

P is for Passive Income

Passive income is probably the best income you can earn.

Here are the three incomes recognized by the Internal Revenue Service (IRS).

> - *Ordinary Income (O)* – income earned by going to work and collecting a paycheck. This income is taxed the most.
> - *Portfolio Income (P)* – income earned by investing; usually investing in stocks, bonds, and other financial assets/paper assets. This income is usually taxed at a Capital Gains rate that is much lower than the Ordinary Income rate.
> - *Passive Income (P)* – income earned usually by owning rental property or real estate or being a limited partner in a business. This income is usually not taxed at all. Hi Trump 😊

Your income will fall into one of those income classes. O.P.P…"Yeah, you know me".

Which income do you think is the best income to earn? That's right! Passive Income, because it is taxed the least.

Q is for Quick Ratio

Quick Ratio is a metric that measures a company's ability to pay its short-term liabilities with its assets. Do you know what a liability is?

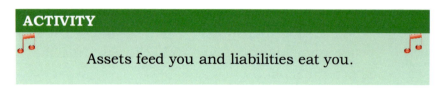

ACTIVITY

♪ Assets feed you and liabilities eat you. ♪

The Quick Ratio metric will determine if a company has enough assets to pay its bills quickly.

Tip!
- Budget your money
- Save your money
- Invest your money
- Repeat

R is for Roblox (joking again!)
R is for Real Estate

Real estate is an asset class that everyone has been involved with in some form or fashion. You need somewhere to live, right? Whether it's a house, condo, apartment, shelter, etc. someone owns that real estate. Real estate is probably the most powerful asset to own because of the tax benefits (see P).

BONUS! *R is for Risk*

In simple terms, risks are threats that can impact your initial cash that is used to buy an asset. There are lots of risks involved when it comes to investing. A lot of people do not invest because of the fear of losing money. This is why financial education is so important because the best way to defeat a risk is to get knowledgeable about investing.

DOUBLE BONUS! *R is for Rate of Return (RoR)*

RoR is the gain from your initial cash or investment over a time period. This calculation is shown using a %.

EXAMPLE: *You invest $120 in an asset like a stock. Let's say Walmart Stock; you hold this stock for one year and sell it at $200 a share. Your gain is $80; $200-120 = $80. Now to determine the % we simply take the gain of $80 and divide it by the initial investment of $120 = 67%. So, in this example you would have a rate of return of 67%.*

Here's a breakdown of the different markets and their overall returns on average per year over the last 30 years:

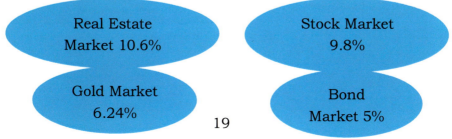

S is for S&P 500

The S&P 500 is an index that measures the world's biggest 500 companies. Think of names like Apple, Facebook, Google, Nike, Disney, Amazon, Exxon, AT&T, Walmart, Tesla, etc. When you hear someone say "the stock market is up" they are referencing the DOW Jones (which is another index that measures only 30 companies) or the S&P 500.

BONUS! S IS FOR SALES

Savings, Savings, and Savings. You must develop a way to delay gratification. In other words, don't buy things just because you want them. Instead of buying Jordan's, use the money you saved from not buying the Jordan's and invest the savings. Increasing your savings is a critical building block in building financial freedom.

BONUS! S IS FOR SALES

Sales are essential, not only for business purposes but everyday life. Think about it like this; you are constantly selling yourself by applying for jobs, meeting new friends, raising funds for your church, your school, etc. If Apple can no longer sell the iPhone, iPad, and other products then this company goes out of business.

TIP

TWO THINGS NEEDED TO BE A GOOD SALESPERSON:

KNOWLEDGE
be knowledgeable about whatever you are selling. Try to learn as much as you possibly can.

CONFIDENCE
the more knowledge you have about whatever you are selling, the more confident you will be and confidence will help you sell more.

T is for Taxes

Taxes are basically fees that people and companies are forced to pay, for earning money.

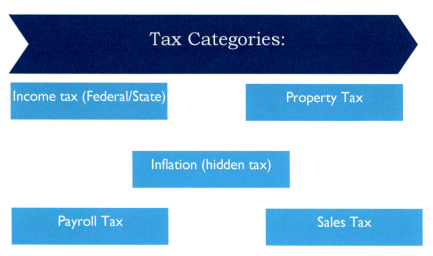

The Internal Revenue Service (IRS) is in charge of making sure taxes are completed accurately and paid on time. Understanding how taxes work is a must if you want gain financial freedom.

Example:

You made $50,000 for the year from working. Well the IRS says "oh goodie" you made a lot of money but we want our money from you. So, the first cut belongs to the Feds, then the state takes their cut, then sales and payroll takes their cut. After all the taxes are paid, all you have left is $25,000. You must learn how to legally keep the IRS from taking your income (see P).

U is for Unicorn

Unicorn is a term used to describe a privately held company. Do you know what a privately held company is? A privately held company stock is not available to buy in the public stock market like Google or Zoom. A private company that has a value of at least $1 billion or more is called a Unicorn.

Examples of Unicorn companies would include: Airbnb and WeWork.

It's awesome to identify young, quality, and good companies before they enter into the public market because you can really make a lot of money investing in them at the Unicorn stage.

V is for Value

Value is the assessment worth of an asset, good, or service. As an investor, it is your duty to try to find the true value of the asset that you want to buy.

If you want to buy real estate, how do you know what price to pay? If you want to buy a stock, how do you know what price to pay? An asset could be overvalued, meaning it might **not** be a good time to buy, or an asset could be undervalued, meaning it's a **good** time to buy. Think of it like this…if you go to the mall and see your favorite pair of shoes on sale for half off it would make sense to buy the shoes at that time. Versus paying full price.

There are several metrics used to determine the value for an asset. You will always need to balance the true value of an asset and what price to pay for it.

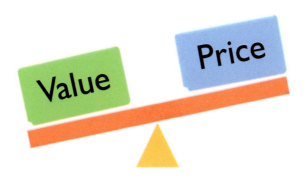

W is for Wall Street

Wall Street is an actual street in New York City, but the name Wall Street is now synonymous with all financial markets. Wall Street can be a name to describe big banks (like JP Morgan, Citi, etc.) or to describe "big business" altogether.

X is for XOM

XOM is the stock symbol for ExxonMobil. Exxon is one of the many oil companies that was created from the original company Standard Oil. The government forced Standard Oil to break up thus Exxon, Chevron, Marathon, and others were formed. If you put the companies back together again, you will have one of the largest, if not largest, oil company in the world.

Below is the breakdown of Standard Oil and all of the baby oil companies to come after it:

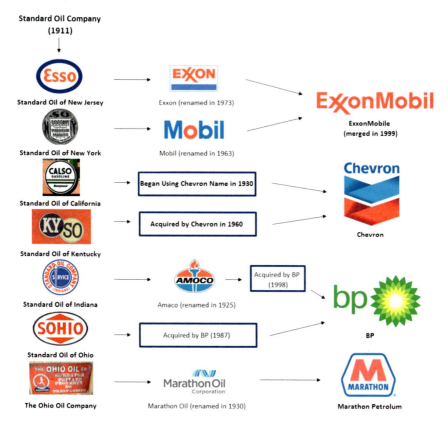

Y is for Yield

Yield is another term for Rate of Return (see R). Your return on your investment is so important we wanted to give you the definition again. It's the money made on an investment over a time period, expressed as a %.

Z is for Zero Sum Game

Zero Sum Game is a term used to describe an investment scenario between two or more people. One person wins and one person loses, but the net wealth of the investment doesn't change.

EXAMPLE: *If I sold you stock after I lost 20% but when you buy the stock, it increases by 20%, the wealth in the overall economy didn't disappear by 20%. It just changed from me to you by 20%. So, there was a zero sum increase in wealth.*

The ABC's of Financial Education

Review:

1. An asset is good to own.
   ○ True   ○ False

2. Passive income is the best income to have.
   ○ True   ○ False

3. Confidence is needed to be a good salesperson.
   ○ True   ○ False

4. Rate of return and yield are the same thing.
   ○ True   ○ False

5. Bad debt is good to have.
   ○ True   ○ False

6. Gold is fake money.
   ○ True   ○ False

The ABC's of Financial Education

Crossword Puzzle

```
E W N A T D T R I I
C G O B S E L N A N
O S E L G S F O S V
N D K D F L E E G E
O C U S A H X T A S
M B H T I A S Y S T
Y P I E T R G A B O
O O E M O C N I C R
N S A V I N G S K D
V A L U E W Z B T Q
```

ASSETS
BUDGET
CASHFLOW
DEBT
ECONOMY
GOLD
INCOME
INFLATION
INVESTOR
RISKS
SAVINGS
TAXES
VALUE

Thank You For Your Purchase!

For comments, questions, feedback, or to join our Listserv please email us at newlevelbooks2@gmail.com

Newlevelbooks2

New Level Books

New Level Books

New Level Books